Managing Behaviour in Classrooms

Managing Behaviour in Classrooms

John Visser

David Fulton Publishers

London

David Fulton Publishers Ltd
Ormond House, 26–27 Boswell Street. London WC1N 3JZ
www.fultonpublishers.co.uk

First published in Great Britain by David Fulton Publishers 2000

Note: The right of John Visser to be identified as the author of this work
has been asserted by him in accordance with the Copyright, Designs and
Patents Act 1988.

British Library Cataloguing in Publication Data
A catalogue record for this book is available from the British Library.

ISBN1–85346–587–9

Typeset by Book Production Services, London
Printed in Great Britain by The Cromwell Press Ltd, Trowbridge, Wilts.

Contents

Foreword

Each publication in this series of books is concerned with approaches to intervention with children with specific needs in mainstream schools. In this foreword we provide a backdrop of general issues concerning special needs in mainstream schools. The government's Action Programme, published after considering responses to the Special Education Needs (SEN) Green Paper, will lead to changes in practice in the future. Following consultation, there will be a revised and simplified Code of Practice in place by the school year 2000/2001. It is intended that this will make life simpler.

The SEN Code of Practice (DfE,1994a), following the 1993 Education Act, provides practical guidance to LEAs and school governing bodies on their responsibilities towards pupils with SEN. Schools and LEAs were required to regard its recommendations from September 1994. The Department for Education also issued Circular 6/94 (DfE 1994b) which provided suggestions as to how schools should manage their special needs provision alongside that made by other local schools. These documents embody the twin strategies of individual pupil support and whole-school development. The Green Paper *Excellence for All* also seeks to promote the development of more sophisticated and comprehensive forms of regional and local planning (DfEE 1997).

The Code of Practice, with its staged approach to assessment supervised within each mainstream school by a teacher designated as Special Educational Needs Coordinator (SENCO), was widely welcomed.

For example, Walters (1994) argued that 'this Code of Practice builds on good practice developed over the ten years and heralds a "new deal" for children with special needs in the schools of England and Wales'. But he also reflected worries that, in the light of other developments, the process might provide an added incentive for schools to dump their 'problem children into the lap of the LEA' rather than devising strategies to improve behaviour in the school environment. Such children, he feared, were in danger of being increasingly marginalised.

Impact on Teachers

While receiving a mainly positive welcome for its intentions, the *Code of Practice* (DfE, 1994a) also raised some concerns about its impact on teachers, who became responsible for its implementation. On the positive side the Code would raise the profile of special needs and establish a continuum of provision in mainstream schools. There was a clear specification of different types of special educational need and the Code's emphasis was on meeting them through individual programmes developed in cooperation with parents.

However, there were possible problems in meeting the challenge of establishing effective and time-efficient procedures for assessment and monitoring. Further challenges were to be found in making best use of resources and overcoming barriers to liaison with parents.

Anxieties about the Code

Following the introduction of the Code these anxieties were confirmed by a number of research studies of teachers' perceptions of the impact of the Code. The picture, which emerged from these studies showed appreciation of the potential benefits of implementing the Code but widespread anxiety, based on early experience, about the practicalities of making it work.

Loxley and Bines (1995) interviewed head teachers and SENCOs about their views on emergent issues related to the complexities of introducing Individual Education Plans (IEPs), particularly in secondary schools.

Teachers feared that 'excessive proceduralism' could lead to the distribution of resources being skewed towards meeting the needs of children whose parents are best able to understand and exercise their rights, at the expense of provision for children whose parents are less assertive and confident. Teachers were most concerned about the allocation of scarce resources and the increased responsibilities of SENCOs for managing a system likely to reduce time for direct teaching of children.

School perspectives

Most schools were optimistic about their ability to implement the Code and positive about LEA guidelines and training, but there was less certainty that the Code would improve the education of pupils with SEN.

Asked to give their opinion on advantages and disadvantages of the Code, teachers cited as positive effects:

- a more structured framework,
- growing awareness of accountability,
- a higher profile for SEN issues,
- earlier identification,
- greater uniformity in practice, and
- increased parental involvement.

The disadvantages cited were:

- lack of resources and time,
- substantially increased workloads for all teachers as well as SENCOs,
- more time used for liaison and less for teaching.

(Rhodes, 1996)

Four themes

A national survey commissioned by the National Union of Teachers (NUT) identified four themes:

1. broad support for the principles and establishment of the Code of Practice;
2. concern about the feasibility of its implementation, given a lack of time and resources;
3. problems in some areas related to perceived inadequacy of LEA support;
4. inadequate status and lack of recognition for the SENCO role.

(Lewis, *et al.* 1996)

Another study found patchy support for SENCOs. There were wide variations in the amount of time dedicated to the role, the amount of support from head teachers and governors, involvement in decision-making, the extent of training and the degree of bureaucracy within LEAs.

SEN Register and Staged Assessment Procedures

Although its widespread adoption makes it appear to have been a national prescription, the five-stage model suggested in the Code is not a legal requirement. The Code actually states that : 'to give specific help to children who have special educational needs, schools should adopt a staged response'. (DfE 1994a, 2.20)

It goes on to indicate that some schools and LEAS may adopt different models but that, while it was not essential that there should be five stages, it was essential that there should be differentiation between the stages, aimed at matching action taken to the pupil's needs at each stage.

Five Key Stages

Nonetheless, the normal expectation is that assessment and intervention will be organised and recorded in an SEN Register for which the SENCO is responsible. The following description briefly summarises usual practice, with stages 1–3 school-based and Stages 4 and 5 the responsibility of the LEA.

Stage 1
Class teacher identifies pupils with learning difficulty and, with support from the SENCO, attempts to meet the pupil's SEN.

Stage 2
Class teacher reports continued concern and SENCO takes responsibility for the special response to meet the pupil's SEN.

Stage 3
SENCO organises support from external agencies to help in meeting the pupil's SEN.

Stage 4
LEA is approached by the school with a request for statutory assessment.

Stage 5
LEA considers the need for a Statement of SEN and completes the assessment procedure; monitoring and review of the statement is organised by the LEA.

Each book in this series, explains how this process works in relation to different disabilities and difficulties as they were described in the 1981 Act and shows how individual needs can be identified and met through IEPs. While forthcoming revision of the Code may alter the details of the stages, the principles of the practices through which needs are specified will remain the same.

Information for colleagues, governors and parents

Ensuring that the school provides all necessary information for staff, governors and parents is another major element of the SENCO role. *The Organisation of Special Educational Provision* (Circular 6/94) (DfE 1994b) sets out the issues which the school should address about its SEN provision, policies and partnerships with bodies beyond the school.

This is information that must be made available and may be found in school brochures or prospectuses, in annual reports to parents and in policy documents. The ultimate responsibility for following the guidance in the Circular rests with the head teacher and governing body but the SENCO will be engaged with all these issues and the Circular forms in effect a useful checklist for monitoring the development and implementation of the SEN policy.

You may find it useful to consider the following points as a way of familiarising yourself with provision in your school.

Basic Information about the school's special educational provision

- Who is responsible for coordinating the day-to-day provision of education for pupils with SEN at your school (whether or not the person is known as the SEN Coordinator)?
- Arrangements need to be made for coordinating the provision of education for pupils with SEN. Does your school's SENCO work alone or is there a coordinating or support team?
- What are the admission arrangements for pupils with SEN who do not have a statement and is there any priority for SEN admissions?
- What kind of provision does your school have for the special educational needs in which it specialises?
- What are you school's access arrangements for pupils with physical and sensory disabilities?

Information about the school's policies for the identification, assessment and provision for all pupils with SEN

- What is your school policy on allocation of money for SEN resources?
- How are pupils with SEN identified and their needs determined and reviewed? How are parents told about this?
- What does your school policy say about arrangements for providing access for pupils with SEN to a balanced and broadly-based curriculum (including the National Curriculum)?
- What does your school policy say about 'integration arrangements'? How do pupils with SEN engage in the activities of the school together with pupils who do not have special educational needs.
- How does your school demonstrate the effective implementation of its SEN policy? How does the governing body evaluate the success of the education which is provided at the school for pupils with SEN?
- What are the arrangements made by the governing body relating to the treatment of complaints from parents of pupils with SEN concerning the provision made at school?
- What are your school's 'time targets' for responses to complaints?

Information about the school's staffing policies and partnership with bodies beyond the school

- What is your school's policy on continuing in-service professional training for staff in relation to special educational needs?
- What are your school's arrangements regarding the use of teachers and facilities from outside the school, including links with support services for special educational needs?
- What is the role played by the parents of pupils with SEN? Is there a 'close working relationship'?
- Do you have any links with other schools, including special schools, and is there provision made for the transition of pupils with SEN between schools or between the school and the next stage of life or education?
- How well does 'Liaison and information exchange' work in your school, e.g. links with health services, social services and educational welfare services and any voluntary organisations which work on behalf of children with SEN?

In any school those arrangements which are generally available to meet children's learning needs will have an impact on those services which are required to meet specific needs. It is therefore very important that a reader of any one of this series of specialist books makes reference to the general situation in their school when thinking about ways of improving the learning situation for pupils.

Harry Daniels and Colin Smith
University of Birmingham
February 1999

Bibliography

Crowther, D., Dyson, A. *et al.* (1997) *Implementation of the Code of Practice: The Role of the Special Educational Needs Co-ordinator.* Special Needs Research Centre, Department of Education, University of Newcastle upon Tyne.

Department for Education (DfE) (1994a) *Code of Practice on the Identification and Assessment of Special Educational Needs.* London: HMSO.

Department for Education (DfE) (1994b) *The Organisation of Special Educational Provision.* Circular 6/94. London: HMSO.

Department for Education and Employment (DfEE) (1997) *Excellence for All: Meeting Special Educational Needs.* London: HMSO.

Hornby, G. (1995) 'The Code of Practice: boon or burden', *British Journal of Special Education.* **22**, 3, 116–119.

Lewis, A., Neill, S. R. St J. and Campbell, R .J. (1996) *The Implementation of the Code of Practice in Primary and Secondary School: A National Survey of the Perceptions of Special Educational Needs Co-ordinators.* The University of Warwick.

Loxley, A. and Bines, H. (1995) 'Implementing the Code of Practice: professional responses', *Support for Learning.* **10**, 4, 185–189.

Rhodes, L. W. (1996) 'Code of Practice: first impressions', *Special!* Spring, 1996.

Walters, B. (1994) *Management of Special Needs.* London: Cassell.

Preface

Books on classroom management abound in the catalogues of publishers, and I trust that it is with humility that I add to that number. This book is based upon a perspective which suggests that there are no easy answers to achieving the well-managed classroom and to working with pupils with emotional and behavioural difficulties, whether these are 'mild' or 'severe'. Nor are there any ready-made prescriptive ones. Rather there are some underlying principles which can be applied in a variety of ways, to meet the diversity of situations and learning needs to be found in classrooms.

This book is a personal perspective based upon the author's experience in primary, secondary and specialist provision as teacher, researcher and consultant. This experience has been shaped by the many teachers and pupils with whom the author has worked. Their responses, contributions and positive criticism have enabled him to improve his professional skills in managing behaviour in classrooms. In particular the questioning, debate and suggestions arising from working with Harry Daniels and Ted Cole have been a valuable contribution to this development.

This book is dedicated to Emma, who put so much of what it contains into her practice, and her brother Andrew, both of whom enhanced my skills as parent and teacher.

John Visser
Birmingham
August 2000

Introduction

This book is written for beginning teachers, those in initial training and in their early years of teaching. It may, as well, be of use to those who seek to refresh their professional skills after teaching for a number of years.

The contents do not seek to address the teaching needs of pupils whose emotional and behavioural difficulties (EBD) are such that they require specialist provision. Rather it seeks to address, within the constraints of a volume, the range of behaviours from the every day 'wear and tear' challenges which teachers face in their teaching to those pupils with EBD whose learning needs can be met within a mainstream school. In managing these behaviours teachers provide teaching environments which enable many children and young people with EBD to cope successfully with school, and to engage in academic learning. When teachers do not successfully manage behaviour in classrooms then the emotional and behavioural difficulties experienced by pupils may be exacerbated to the point where both they and their teachers feel they can no longer cope and alternative provision is required.

The book is not aimed at teachers of a particular age group. It is not the age or stage which is a key factor in successful management of behaviour. What is important is teachers' understanding of how the age of the pupil affects their implementation of the ideas the book contains. The characteristics of good classroom management are the same whatever the age taught. It is the manner and varying emphasis in which they are applied in practice with different groups which differ.

While reading the book the reader will find it useful to have in mind a group of pupils with whom he or she is familiar. Reflecting, with this group in mind, upon the application of the ideas it contains, will provide the reader with a point of reference with which to test their validity and applicability to successfully managing behaviour in the classroom.

The ideas contained here are not put forward in any absolute sense. The book is not a prescription to be followed in a regimented way. The author has found that not all the ideas it contains will work all of the time for all teachers with all pupils. Managing classes, like any human activity, involves an almost infinite number of variables. This variety presents an endless possible set of combinations. Each classroom presents a fresh challenge in managing behaviour, requiring flexibility in the application of strategies to meet the uniqueness contained within the commonalities that exist in teaching and learning.

Some underlying common characteristics emerge from teachers' experiences and research that are associated with teachers who manage classrooms successfully. These characteristics (based upon Daniels *et al.* 1998) are:

- a professional attitude to teaching;
- a consistency of approach;
- a flexibility and responsiveness with individuals;
- evidenced-based teaching;
- a belief in including all children in their teaching.

This book attempts to illustrate and develop these characteristics.

CHAPTER 1

Why manage behaviour in classrooms?

Teachers need to have the skills of good management behaviour within classrooms for the following reasons:

- it provides a structure for academic learning;
- it does not occur spontaneously;
- it provides for greater job satisfaction;
- it provides pupils with models of acceptable social behaviour.

Good classroom behaviour is not achieved by default, it does not just happen. Once individuals have been placed into groups, some form of leadership is needed which manages the purpose for the grouping. The teacher must provide this leadership or it will emerge from within the group. The purpose for the group is reflected in the leadership provided. So managing the behaviour in the classroom is *de facto* a part of being a teacher if the purpose of the group is to engage in learning managed by a teacher. In extremes, should pupils entirely take over the leadership of the group, one can be fairly certain that the purpose for the group will bear little relationship to academic achievements along the lines of the national curriculum.

What is important is the form of leadership the teacher provides. Successful leadership will need to take cognisance of the cultural norms pervading within the community. Hence in twenty-first century England an authoritarian approach to managing classroom behaviours will meet more resistance than it did when society was more overtly hierarchical, and 'authority' an aspect of that class structure. The opposite extreme, that of adopting a 'laissez-faire' approach which is directionless, with no purpose or form, is equally out of place at a period when targets, competencies, national tests and examinations are the major goals of education. The best leadership provided by teachers is somewhere between these two extremes. It has a sense of purpose, a degree of negotiation and enables progression, which combine to give a sense of achievement for all concerned. In this form of leadership it is particularly important for teachers to form positive relationships with pupils.

Teaching and learning is a managed series of relationships between teacher and taught. The better managed the relationship the greater the satisfaction for the teacher in a job well done, and the greater the learners' achievements. Among the factors which contribute to positive relationships between teachers and pupils are:

- good subject knowledge;
- high expectations for pupils' achievement;
- lively, well-paced lessons;
- ensuring all pupils' learning needs are met;
- acting upon evidence from teaching and learning to inform future teaching;
- high standards of classroom management.

These factors have been listed separately but are closely intertwined and overlapping. In the well-managed classroom the teacher is constantly interacting with pupils across all these factors. Behaviour and classroom management is not a factor which can be separated entirely from the other factors. Indeed, behaviour is not separate from learning; it can be argued that learning is a behaviour.

Classrooms are groups of pupils whose time is structured by a teacher around academic learning. Pupils' use of time during other aspects of their school day is often referred to as unstructured; observe the school playground or the lunch break to see pupils operating in ways which are not structured by the teacher. Managing behaviour is part of the structure that the teacher provides, to be supportive and directive of pupil's learning.

The structure provides a context which supports the purpose for the lesson and its importance. The manner in which teachers manage the behaviour in their classrooms gives messages to the pupils regarding their beliefs, values and attitudes. In particular these messages convey:

- the strength of belief in the importance of the task;
- their attitude towards individual pupils;
- the valuing of individual achievement.

These factors set the context in which pupils' behaviour takes place. The structure also models and provides parameters for the behaviour the teacher expects from pupils.

A final pertinent reason for managing behaviour is the prevention of poor behaviour which disrupts academic learning. Prevention in this instant is much easier than cure. The well-managed classroom provides pupils with that sense of security of purpose which enables them to make progress. Classrooms without teacher-managed behaviour tend to be chaotic places where little academic learning takes place, where teachers' stress levels are high and pupils' insecurities give rise to inappropriate behaviours.

CHAPTER 2
Pupils who challenge

Few pupils challenge their teachers. Most pupils, in almost all classrooms, for nearly all of the time, are willing to develop the necessary social skills to understand and enact the 'rules of engagement' in the classroom.

However, even in the best-managed classrooms pupils will, from time to time, present teachers with behaviours which challenge. These challenges can take many forms and, though often signalled well in advance, can also happen very abruptly. For some pupils the better managed the classroom the safer it is to misbehave. For others, particularly in the early stages of a pupil–teacher relationship, the challenges can be a test to ascertain what the boundaries of toleration are.

Usually, while the behaviour which challenges is directed at teachers, it may not be caused by them. Pupils come into classrooms from a variety of backgrounds: some supportive of schooling, others not so supportive; some with well-developed appropriate social skills for their age, others less so; some from emotionally secure backgrounds, others from emotionally volatile contexts. These and other factors can mean that the pupil's own emotional and behavioural state for a period of time are such that he or she feels resentful, angry, hurt, frustrated, revengeful to name but a few possible characteristics. Merely by being there on that occasion the teacher may bear the brunt of the outburst. If it happens repeatedly over time, advice from a specialist teacher of pupils with EBD may be necessary. But what can be done in the meantime?

- avoid scapegoating;
- check the SEN register;
- be aware of the IEP and PSP;
- record the challenges;
- plan your reaction to challenge.

Scapegoating

Within schools from time to time a folklore among staff can emerge which identifies a pupil or group of pupils as the behavioural challenge of all time. Living in a certain street or estate, even coming from a particular family is often used as an identifier. Once identified and 'labelled', levels of expectation of challenging behaviours from the pupil are created, and the pupil's behaviour is interpreted by reference to the labels. It leads to comments by teachers such as 'well what do you expect, he's a …'. It is important to be wary of such scapegoating. Pupils are seldom so challenging that their behaviour is poor for all teachers. In her study of pupils in a comprehensive school, Morris (1999) found that even pupils with severe behaviour difficulties, who were eventually permanently excluded, behaved well for some teachers within the school. When faced with the challenging pupil it might be useful to reflect upon for whom within the school that pupil is not a challenge and to discuss with them why. Their insights may be useful in defusing the challenges a pupil presents.

The avoidance of scapegoating can be difficult, as it may be very entrenched in the discourse of the staffroom. Scapegoating can be counteracted by recognising the individuality of the pupil(s) involved. In doing so the pupil's strengths (things they can and do perform well) may emerge. For example, they may have social skills which can be utilised by the teacher in managing the classroom, often by being given a simple task which assigns some status and value. Thus the challenge from the pupil may be diverted to positive effect.

The SEN register and IEPs

All schools in England and Wales have a register of pupils with special educational needs (SEN). In Scotland and Northern Ireland similar records are kept. This is usually kept and regularly updated by the school's special educational needs coordinator (SENCO). The register will have details of pupils' learning needs, and should also contain information regarding any emotional and behavioural difficulties they are experiencing. These details will give rise to an individual education plan (IEP), which will set short-term learning targets for staff to incorporate into their teaching. The IEP may have teaching suggestions enabling pupils to achieve these targets. Learning in this instance may also cover behaviour: targets for learning the necessary social skills to engage in classroom learning. Teachers need to ensure that they are aware of pupils on the SEN register who are in their classes. The pupils' IEPs must be incorporated into lesson plans. (See Cornwall and Tod 1998 for a detailed exposition of IEPs for pupils with emotional and behavioural difficulties.)

Recording challenges and the PSP

Keep a note of the times when a pupil or pupils are challenging. Records should include brief details of who, what and how. Who was involved, what was the challenge and how did it happen. This will build an evidence base upon which to develop strategies which can be implemented, reviewed and revised to meet the challenges and reduce their incidence. Working from an evidence base will avoid the 'negative labelling' which arises from constantly moaning about a pupil to the point where everything about the pupil is perceived as wrong. Isolating the incidents of challenge should also alert the teacher to the occasions when the pupil does not challenge, is working, making progress, behaving and can be appropriately praised.

Circular 10/99 (DfEE 1999), *Social Inclusion: Pupil Support,* gives guidance to schools on Pupil Support Plans (PSPs). Arising from the Government's concern over the rising number of school exclusions in the late 1990s, PSPs were suggested as a way of enabling schools to identify pupils whose behaviour, rather than their learning, was the cause of concern. It is rarely the case that a pupil whose behaviour is of concern is fulfilling their academic learning potential. However, it may be that a school wishes to ensure that it is working both on behaviour and academic learning issues and thus a PSP can be viewed as complementary to an IEP. The PSP should contain details of what the behavioural needs are and what strategies are being applied to address these needs. Good PSPs will address these through teaching strategies whose aim is to re-engage or sustain and develop the engagement of the pupil in his or her learning.

Planning the reaction to challenge

When challenged by a pupil, the teacher's reaction can contribute to an escalation or de-escalation of the challenge. There are strategies which can de-escalate the challenge. They need to be planned for. The teacher who has thought the strategies through beforehand and has them as part of his or her teaching skills is in a better position than teachers who, when the challenge occurs, react instinctively. The instinctive feelings aroused by challenge, particularly to a teacher's sense of authority, are those of threat, insecurity, heightened stress and feelings of incompetence, none of which may be true; however, these emotions are as powerful for teachers as for pupils. The instinctive reactions to these feelings are in the range of 'flight or fight' and can lead to an escalation of the challenge. Any escalation is damaging to the pupil and teacher relationship, the cornerstone of teaching and learning.

When challenged:

- remember it is not always personal;
- try to isolate the incident;
- listen to the pupil;
- contextualise your decision;
- re-establish the task.

Remember it is not always personal

As outlined above, while the challenge may be directed at you, it may not be caused by you. The incident can have a variety of causes of which you *may* be a small, inadvertent, part. React calmly with firmness. Let the pupil be aware that you know there is a challenge by addressing the issue immediately. A reaction which does not convey calm firmness will lead to an escalation of the situation. A loud authoritarian stance seldom brings the pupil to his or her senses. The quiet recognition gives the pupil a message that the teacher is aware of the situation. It also gives the teacher time to decide if the matter needs a greater degree of intervention.

Try to isolate the incident

Challenging behaviour most frequently occurs in group situations, where others can be involved. Their involvement can broaden and deepen the challenge for the teacher. The sooner the challenge can be isolated, the more quickly it can be resolved.

Isolation in this sense does not only mean isolating the pupil by removing them from the situation. This can often be helpful, giving the pupil an opportunity to calm down; it avoids audience participation and can enable other pupils to continue with their learning. However, it can also cause resentment, with the pupil festering on the issues while they are removed from the situation. The pupil may feel that an injustice has occurred. The teacher may have seen him or her as the challenge when others may have been the initiators. Thus isolating the pupil needs careful consideration, and should only be for a very short duration.

Isolate the incident, without removing the pupil, by dealing with it quickly and firmly, and moving the lesson on, perhaps by reiterating the task or changing the activity. By maintaining the pace of the lesson, the incident can be seen as being nothing more than a small blip in the progress the teacher and the class are making. It can also ensure that molehills do not become mountains. Occasionally this can be achieved by ignoring the incident, whilst logging it in the teacher's mind to be dealt with quietly later. A quick acknowledgement and then moving straight on with the lesson, perhaps setting a task to be completed can be effective. This may involve comments such as 'what you have just said/done is not very appropriate. I will talk with you later about it. For now can we all get on with ….'. Such an isolating strategy conveys an understanding to the pupil of the teacher's awareness of the incident and willingness to deal with it, while stressing the importance of achieving the learning tasks set for the lesson.

Listen to the pupil

Challenging behaviour within the classroom has causes which can lie in four possible areas: lack of understanding; a sense of injustice; a desire to vent feelings of anger, frustration and powerlessness in an inappropriate manner; and a lack of motivation towards the task. (These in turn have a larger set of possible causes.) The pupil will genuinely experience these feelings, even if inappropriately so. Telling a pupil that he or she has no right to feel, think or act in such a manner during the heat of the incident will do little to convey the teacher's understanding and sense of value for the pupil. It is important to acknowledge pupils' feelings especially when they challenge – it may even be a revelation to them. Acknowledging their upset, anger and frustration can often stop them in their tracks, and the recognition can lessen the need to express the feelings in such forceful ways. The pupil may not have an understanding of the link between the reaction they are causing by their behaviour and their legitimately held feeling.

Having acknowledged the feelings, it then becomes important to provide a time for pupils to explain their feelings. This may not be immediately, not only because the lesson needs to continue for all the pupils, but also because a degree of privacy may be a prerequisite if the pupil is to feel secure in saying what he or she is feeling and why. It is not always easy for the pupil to acknowledge, for example, that he or she is completely lost in the lesson, let alone other more personal matters such as feeling isolated, bullied and threatened. Tell the pupil that you are aware, for example, that they feel angry and will discuss it with them at a set time, perhaps after the lesson or during a break time.

Remember, however, that a discussion has two parts, speaking and listening. Too often 'discussion', as far as the pupil is concerned, means teachers talking *at* rather than *with* them and the teacher doing nearly all the talking. Listening to pupils is an important stage in resolving challenging behaviours.

Listening conveys acknowledgement and value, but it does not of itself convey approval for the behaviour. It provides the teacher with insights into why the behaviour occurred and what might possibly be done in future to avoid the need for the behaviour. Strategies for use by both pupil and teacher may emerge which enable the pupil to feel that he or she have both a responsibility for the behaviour and its effects, as well as the potential to change that behaviour for one that is more socially acceptable.

When listening to pupils, teachers may need to use prompting questions, to enable the pupil to articulate his or her understanding of the event. 'What happened' questions can establish the sequence of events and point to the possible 'trigger' which invoked the behaviour, leading to questions such as 'What were you feeling', which can establish the emotional state of the pupil. Avoid 'why' questions, they tend to evoke the response 'because', which leads to placing the responsibility for the incident and resultant behaviour outside the control of the pupil. The typical answer to the question 'Why did you ...' is the response 'Because he/she/it/they made me'.

This can mean 'I am not in charge of my behaviour and it is somebody else you need to change, not me'. Whereas questions which provoke what other responses could have been made by the pupil give the opportunity to explore alternative behaviours and responses. Questions relating to what responses would be chosen in similar events, and checks on how they now view the incident, can enable pupils to realise that there are alternative ways of dealing with what are often legitimate feelings of anger, frustration and powerlessness.

Contextualise your decision

Beside the comment that 'teachers do not listen' many pupils also remark that 'teachers make arbitrary decisions'. By the latter they can mean that they do not see any logic or reason for the decision made. Decisions made by teachers are nearly always based on sound professional reasoning. They have usually been arrived at after considering a variety of factors and coming to a balanced view. However, often all the pupil receives is the decision; the reasons for it are not always explicit.

Explaining, however briefly, the reasons for a decision can provide pupils with the sense that there is a logic to it. It can also convey a sense that the teacher has taken them and others into consideration in making the decision. Such explanations give the pupil a context in which to place their behaviour and the outcomes that derive from it, enabling them to gain understanding of cause and effect in terms of behaviour.

Re-establish the task

Challenging behaviour is unsettling for the pupil, his or her class, and for the teacher. It is disruptive of the smooth flow and pace of the lesson and interrupts the working relationship. Re-establishing that working relationship as soon as a challenging incident has occurred is important. It re-focuses the pupil upon the importance of the learning task, and settles him or her back into the routines of learning. Getting the pupil back on task also helps to convey the sense that though the teacher is angry or concerned about the behaviour, the pupil remains valued because he or she is able to engage in the learning. It is important when doing this to check that the pupil understands what is required, and that task completion is within his or her grasp. Asking the pupil to explain what he or she believes is required can provide an opportunity to explore any misunderstanding about the task, as well as a check that the pupil has the skills, knowledge and/or understanding necessary to re-engage in the task.

CHAPTER 3

Pupils with emotional and behavioural difficulties

Pupils with emotional and behavioural difficulties (EBD) have a special education need and should be on the school's register of special education need. The identification and assessment of EBD is problematic. There is widespread, interchangeable and inappropriate use of a broad range of terms to describe pupils with EBD (Daniels *et al.* 1998). This problem of definition gives rise to inconsistent identification of pupils with EBD between, and within, local education authorities and schools. Attempts by Government (DfE 1994, DfEE 1997) and authors (e.g. Cooper 1996, Charlton and David 1993) to define this group do so largely in terms of a continuum of behaviour. This leads to a greater emphasis upon behavioural difficulties and less emphasis upon emotional difficulties (Maras 1996, Bowers 1996, Greenhalgh 1994).

This is important because it can lead to a view of behavioural difficulties as devoid of emotional content, and as emotional difficulties as not having a behavioural consequence that impacts upon teaching and learning. There is evidence (Maras 1996, Bowers 1996, Gray and Richer 1988, DES 1989) that teachers are more concerned about persistent behaviour difficulties and, focusing upon these, overlook those pupils whose EBD is centred upon emotional difficulties. These often manifest in behaviours which are less disruptive to teacher's management of behaviour in the classroom. Nonetheless these behaviours, often of a 'withdrawing' nature, can be as inhibiting of academic progress as behaviours which are overtly challenging.

It is suggested that this is one reason why there is a significant absence of girls in the group labelled EBD, and possibly for the over-representation of pupils from ethnic minority communities, especially those of Afro-Caribbean origin (Cooper *et al.* 1994, McIntyre 1995, Maras 1996, Cole, *et al.* 1998).

Recently there have been indications that future official definitions of these pupils will include 'social' in their title (DfEE 2000). Thus the spectrum will broaden to include those pupils who are currently viewed as merely disaffected and/or disruptive. While this may lead to a further blurring of the defining of EBD, it will draw into the definition in a more overt manner aspects of the social life of pupils which affect their academic progress.

The defining and understanding of EBD by teachers and schools is important because it represents how they delineate between the pupil whose behaviour is seen essentially as naughtiness, infrequent, touching on the mischievous which may occasionally rise to being challenging, and those regarded as having persistent behaviours which are inappropriate for the age and developmental stage of the pupil. As circular 9/94 (DfE 1994, p.4) puts it, EBD lies between:

> behaviour which challenges teachers but is within normal, albeit unacceptable, bounds and that which is indicative of serious mental illness. The distinction between normal but stressed behaviour, emotional and behavioural difficulties and behaviour arising from mental illness is important because each needs to be treated differently.

The circular goes on to outline how this range of behaviours impacts upon pupils' learning, pointing out that these pupils frequently are underachieving and often have learning difficulties. They frequently have disengaged from academic learning. Thus these pupils are seen as having special educational needs (SEN).

A central means of meeting their SEN is the provision of well-managed classrooms. The teacher's standards of behaviour and expectations establishes a goal which pupils with EBD can rise to. They provide a secure purposeful environment which lays the foundation for these pupils to re-engage in their education.

An equally important aspect of understanding, defining and use of the term EBD is its generic and transitory nature. Besides being used to describe a wide and varied set of difficulties, there is a danger that it is perceived of as a permanent condition. It is unfortunately true that a pupil who has been placed in a special school for pupils with EBD will, when those difficulties have diminished or their effect been eradicated, find it difficult to be reincluded in a mainstream school. Too many professionals within education view EBD as a condition (like being left-handed, or severely visually impaired) which is forever there (Cole *et al.* 1998).

Thus it is important for the teacher to realise that the label EBD is useful as a general generic description, but that its ascription to a pupil should lead to that individual having his or her learning needs met. Once met, he or she should no longer be viewed as being a pupil with EBD.

CHAPTER 4

Parents, carers and families

When faced with pupils whose behaviours are disruptive in the classroom it is all too easy to blame the pupils' parents, carers and families for not providing the correct upbringing. This is often based upon a 'rose-tinted' perception of one's own upbringing in which the development of socially acceptable behaviours was the outcome of a stereotypical nuclear family headed by a male with a wife and dependent children. There exists a tendency in education to look back to some golden age when it is believed all families were stable, harmonious groups where children were brought up to be adjusted, happy and well-behaved pupils. While it is true that many of us grew up in a situation where this was the predominant climate, it was not always so and for some children it was rarely so. Families, carers and parents have always varied, and this variety has provided the nurturing environment which has produced both 'saints' and 'sinners'. Further, there appears to be no set formula for parenting which will guarantee the successful, socially adjusted, emerging adult. A reading of biographies and case studies reveals the truth of this (see e.g. Axline 1966, Ashworth, 1998).Pupils come from very diverse backgrounds, families take very different forms and they each have their own validity. They are real and actual for the individual pupil. Teachers may have views on the particular form of family a pupil exists in; however, what is important is that their legitimately held view does not cloud judgements made of the pupil's behaviour. The teacher's task is to provide a classroom in which they can manage behaviours. This task is never easy and may be made more difficult by the behaviours the pupil arrives with; nonetheless it remains one of the key tasks for teachers if their pupils are to engage in academic learning.

It is as well to be aware that some pupils in a class may have to cope with immense personal difficulties. These can range from temporary economic hardship through job loss to looking after a family member who has a severe disability. It could be a parent who is addicted to substance abuse; it could be a violent adult. If it happens in life, then there is a certainty that it happens to pupils in teachers' classes. These life events can have very debilitating effects, making pupils tired, irritable and angry, to mention just a few possibilities. Their reactions to what are trivial events in class may appear extreme unless the teacher understands the family context.

Involving parents and carers in behaviour management is important, particularly for the pupil who challenges. There will be occasions when this is very difficult, if not next to impossible, yet it remains important. Parents and carers may need to be listened to in the same manner described earlier for pupils. What can be key to their involvement is to ensure that they are involved when their child behaves well, as well as when he or she challenges. The experience of many parents is that teachers only contact them as individuals when their child's behaviour is a cause for concern. They, as parents, can often be facing similar challenges from the child, and in some cases they may be the reason for the behaviours. If so, then they will have all the feelings of strain and stress the teacher endures, added to which may be feelings of failing as a parent (even when it is not their 'fault' that their child is challenging). They will rarely have been informed of the occasions when their child has behaved well. Parents and carers can provide powerful reinforcement when they are made aware of the occasions when the pupil behaves well. They will certainly feel less threatened and more rewarded when this is the case. It will also ensure that pupils see teachers and parents/carers working in a partnership.

Working with parents and carers can counteract the teachers' 'counsel of despair': 'There is nothing that I can do because of X's home/parents/environment'. It provides opportunities for teachers to find ways in which pupils' behaviours can be shaped towards the more socially acceptable forms needed for classroom learning. It can also give teachers insights into the ways in which their pupils learn so they can match their teaching strategies to these. Finally, working with parents is but one way in which teachers can and do make a difference to pupils' lives.

Other major 'out of school' factors which could affect pupils' behaviours and need to be understood are cultural, linguistic and poverty factors. Understanding the cultural norms pertaining to some family groupings can help to explain behaviour patterns that teachers observe in their pupils. Linguistic difficulties may be caused by the pupil having English as an additional language to that spoken at home. It may be the case that the range of vocabulary and its use differs from that which is used to promote learning by the teacher, causing misunderstanding as well as a lack of understanding of what is required on the part of the pupil. Poverty in its widest sense can have a grinding down effect which does little to aid motivation in the classroom.

CHAPTER 5

Teachers make a difference

There is a well-researched body of evidence which shows that teachers make a difference in the behaviour of pupils. (For examples see DES 1989, Mortimore *et al.* 1988, Brown and McIntyre 1993, Farrell 1995, Smith and Laslett 1993, Rutter *et al.* 1979.) Beside the factors which the other sections of this book touch upon, there are five aspects of being a teacher which aid the teacher in making this difference. They are:

- knowledge and implementation of policies;
- expectations;
- developing evidence-based practice;
- being a team player;
- knowing and managing yourself.

Knowledge and implementation of policies

Every school should have, and every school in England and Wales must have, a behaviour policy. These are often written by key members of staff, though the best are derived from and agreed by the whole school community: parents, governors, pupils, teachers and support staff. In order to be effective they should be 'lived' documents (Daniels *et al.* 1998): that is, documents which both inform and in turn are informed by the day-to-day practice of managing behaviour in schools and thus in the classroom.

When these documents become set in stone, only to be revisited when an inspection is expected, they are less than useful in supporting staff to attain overall high standards in managing behaviour. These documents should reflect practice, both informing the practice and being informed by the practice. Where practice is seen to deviate from the policy, the questions to be raised should centre upon the need to review both, not to assume automatically that either the practice or the policy is correct and that it is the other which needs to be changed.

These policies often cover a widespread number of issues, from equal opportunities and factors surrounding ethnicity to the school rules and sanctions. They frequently lay out procedures teachers must follow, such as when dealing with major disruptions or when enforcing a particular sanction or dealing with a specific form of unacceptable behaviour such as bullying.

These documents should provide for a consistency of approach by all staff in the school and this is of particular importance where pupils come across a number of staff in the course of a school week. Even in the primary sector, where pupils are with a class teacher for a substantial period of their day, they also are in groups under the supervision of others at times like assembly and break times. The importance of consistency of approach has been touched on earlier and will be returned to later. What is of importance here is that the teacher is familiar with the school policy and incorporates it into his or her practice within the classroom in order to ensure that consistency. It is salutary to note that important sections of a behaviour policy such as the school rules are often not known by the staff, whilst there is an expectation that all pupils obey them. The implications of this state of affairs are many, but importantly the message is that rules only apply to pupils.

Expectations

Teachers have expectations of what a given class of pupils will achieve. They are often implicit and pupils have to ascertain them by the responses they obtain from teachers. Where teachers make them explicit they provide pupils with clear guidance on the standards of behaviour and work which they can rise to. Expectations of achievements need to be realistic, based upon evidence of previous achievements, and set in a way which will meet pupils' need to progress at their maximum possible rate.

Realistic but high expectations of learning provide pupils with the motivation to stay on task. Being on task, besides enabling pupils to learn, provides that all-important sense of making progress which is a powerful motivational force. Pupils when learning need to be locked into a success circle, where success in learning leads to positive feelings as a learner, which in turn enables the pupil to continue with learning. Low teacher expectations, easily achieved and without challenge, lack any motivational force and lead pupils to see the work as a time-filling exercise at best, while at worst their self-esteem as learners falls.

Pupils who have a reputation as being behaviourally difficult, or have been labelled as having EBD, often have their learning needs, if not disregarded, put at a lower priority. Teachers faced with such pupils often resort to giving easier tasks in the belief that easy, means 'do-able' and 'do-able', means 'occupied' and 'occupied', means less tempted to disrupt. This is a false line of logic, in that if a task is easily do-able to the point where it only occupies, it presents no challenge to learn and lowers expectations. It provides for time and energy to be devoted to other activities which may be the breeding grounds of inappropriate and challenging behaviours. In a knowledge–based society an old proverb changed to 'the devil makes work for idle minds' seems to apply to managing behaviour in classrooms. The pupils who are given appropriately challenging tasks are more likely to stay on task as they acquire the sense of self-worth and motivation that comes from achievements which can be recognised by themselves, their teacher and their peers.

Developing evidence-based practice

There are many books (of which this is one) and quite a few staffroom pundits who give advice on the management of behaviour. Not all of them make the cautionary statement this one does in its introduction, that there is no prescription which, if followed to the letter, will produce the perfectly managed classroom. In arriving at well-managed behaviour in the classroom teachers need to develop evidence-based practice based upon their reading, observation and professional activity in the classroom.

Teachers can extend their skills by seeking advice, reading widely and putting strategies into practice. However, in order to gain professionally valid strategies teachers will need to develop evidenced-based practice. To do otherwise is to lurch from one strategy to another with little reasoning as to why one strategy should be preferred in any given situation.

There are a number of ways in which evidence-based practice can be developed. One strategy based upon activity theory (Engestrom 1996, Daniels *et al.* 1998) provides a five-stage strategy in which teachers can develop an evidence base to inform their management of behaviour in the classroom. The five stages are:

1. questioning — what
2. analysing — why

3.   patterns   –   connections
4.   interrogating   –   validating model
5.   implementing   –   putting strategies into practice

The first stage involves identifying an aspect of teaching and learning and then asking questions to identify that aspect in precise terms. For example, what were the factors which led to a particular incident, what did I, as the teacher do, what was the pupil's reactions? What are the differing players' perspectives of the incident? Establishing the widest possible understanding of what occurred gives a firmer basis for the second stage, that of analysis, exploring possible reasons for the interactions between teacher and pupil(s). Why did the interaction proceed in the way it did?

The third stage involves identifying patterns of possible cause and effect. Teaching and learning involves many factors that interact with one another in complex and diverse ways. Any particular incident can be understood differently from the perspective of each of the players. The players in school terms are all those involved and could include pupils, parents, governors, teachers, support staff and learning support assistants. Each will have an understanding of what occurred. The analysis of individuals' understandings can begin to produce data from which a common pattern emerges. Engestrom (1996) calls this stage 'modelling', where the emerging patterns can be diagrammatically represented. Such modelling (Daniels *et al.* in press) provides an easy way of sharing with the players what the teacher believes are the salient features of the aspect of teaching and learning being explored. It is also easy to update a model as understanding progresses and new or different strategies are applied. This is the fourth stage, where with the help of colleagues the model can be interrogated. Discussion, alternative views, different perspectives (see later for an outline of different perspectives on understanding and explaining behaviours) help to 'test' the robustness of the model, giving the teacher a basis upon which to explore ways of identifying those factors within the model which he or she can alter to achieve a different outcome, or can reinforce to maintain a successful outcome already achieved. The fifth stage, that of implementation, is self-evident but of importance in that it leads to further questioning and development of the issues involved.

Though it both reads and sounds like a complex process, it can be as simple as identifying a pupil's inability to remain seated while performing a task: establishing possible reasons why, what triggers the movement, what causes the pupil to be seated when he or she is, then writing down or drawing this in a representational manner and sharing it with colleagues. Following their input, the teacher decides upon alternative strategies to enable the pupil to remain seated and on task. What is important even in this simple example is that the process is a conscious, deliberate one. The teaching strategies adopted are not left to 'intuition', nor are they haphazardly applied with the resultant problems of inconsistency.

Without this form of reflective evidence building to support practice, teachers have to fall back on crisis management of challenging behaviours. Crisis management is a set of reactive behaviours on the teachers' part which is unplanned. Being reactive increases stress levels, tends to produce the same actions from the teacher and thus the same reactions from the pupil(s). Evidence-based teaching provides for a more proactive approach where the teacher can feel in greater control and can explore different approaches before the challenging behaviour arises. It also lessens that sense of isolation many teachers feel when faced with pupils who misbehave: it only happens to me.

Being a team player

Managing behaviour in the classroom can be an isolating experience for teachers. Beside the often unspoken rule that it is not done to mention behaviour challenges in the staffroom, there is always the sense in teaching that the challenging situations which arise are unique to the individual teacher. This is far from true. Whilst there is a uniqueness within each situation, there are also many common points.

Sharing with colleagues one's successful, less successful and unsuccessful strategies should support the development of good classroom management. When teachers feel isolated their potential range of strategies for management narrow to what they also perceive, as an individual, to be possible. They will take fewer risks in experimenting with alternative strategies when faced with challenging behaviour. Good quality teaching is supported by sharing ideas about resources, skills, management and organisation with colleagues. In such sharing, teachers can acquire new strategies, alternative perspectives and perhaps different materials which can be put to use in managing behaviour.

Such 'sharing' experiences can be quite informal and spontaneous, or more formally organised, as in teacher support teams (Creese *et al.* 1997). What is reported by staff involved in these sharing activities is the realisation that they are not alone, and that though there may not be a ready-made solution to the issue there are many possibilities to try out. They also report a lessening of stress and feelings of incompetence.

Knowing and managing yourself

Teaching has many positive satisfying experiences. However, when faced with a difficult class or pupil, there is a tendency not only to forget that they too can provide and be a part of a positive experience for the teacher, but also that the other positive experiences did not take place. Teachers can magnify the difficulties an incident, pupil or class present to the point where their perception of their ability to manage a particular incident is seen as a personal failure. *The Elton Report* (DES 1989) particularly makes mention of the wearing nature of behaviours by pupils and classes which the teacher finds irritating and disruptive. Such classes and pupils can be very draining on the emotional and professional skills of the teacher. This sense of exhaustion can be heightened with a class that you find hard to manage.

This exhaustion is often accompanied by feelings of stress, being threatened, loss of authority and feeling that skills in managing behaviour are under attack and wasting away.

Given the pace of teaching and the range of pressures upon teachers there is often little time for teachers to reflect on the causes of their stress and move to reduce it. This stress will be reflected in the manner in which they approach and cope with their pupils. Being over-stressed has the effect of reducing energy levels, which in turn has a tendency to reduce the liveliness and pace of lessons. Teachers in this state often teach in what they perceive to be safe if unexciting ways. A level of stress, for pupils as well as staff, can be a stimulant to engage in tasks and pursue outcomes seen as worthwhile. Achieving this positive level of stress is important if teachers are to avoid stress levels being a factor in the behaviours that they experience from pupils in class. To achieve it teachers need to ensure that their lives are not totally taken up with education, that they have a good knowledge and understanding of themselves and their own professional behaviours.

The teachers who understand their own behaviours are better equipped to manage the behaviours of pupils in the classroom. Such teachers have a well-developed sense of their own strengths and weaknesses, ensure that they have a 'life' outside education, have one or more critical friends with whom they can share success as well as challenges, and keep a focus upon the progress they and their pupils are making.

CHAPTER 6

Understanding behaviour

Understanding human behaviour is important for teachers who need to manage it, but carries with it a potentially fatal temptation. Understanding behaviour can and should lead teachers to devise ways in which they and their pupils can engage in teaching and learning. Gaining that understanding can also provide teachers with insights into their own behaviours: why they find some behaviour more inappropriate than others and how behaviours are acquired and developed. The fatal temptation is the fascination and seduction the pursuit of these understandings can have in persuading teachers that nothing can be done because of factors which affect behaviour and over which the teacher can have little control. Along with this, particularly when confronted by a particularly intriguing set of behaviours, is the temptation to move away from the task of teaching into the realms of other professionals' tasks, such as social work and counselling. Teachers are there to teach, which involves managing pupils' behaviours and providing sufficient educational care and support to enable pupils to engage or re-engage in learning within the classroom.

Teaching, as a profession, is not social work, psychiatry, juvenile justice nor yet clinical psychology, though professionals in all these areas can affect pupils in schools. Their role with individual pupils will be a part of 'treatment' (see Cole *et al.* 1998 for an explanation of the use of the term 'treatment') of which education is a part. The school's SENCO or senior staff responsible for multi-agency work will have these aspects in hand. Some pupils' needs in areas such as these are so great as to require specialist provision and access to teachers who have specialised in the area of emotional and behavioural difficulties. It is as well to remember, however, that many pupils whose backgrounds can be described in very bleak ways, such that they are in need of the services of the professionals listed above, are in schools and are succeeding academically. Little research has been published on why this is so. What is it that enables one pupil with the same range of disturbing background and within-child factors to succeed, where another appears to fail? Why do some pupils have a greater resilience than others?

The notion of resilience has been investigated by a number of researchers (see e.g. Wang and Reynolds 1995). This research indicates that the building of 'significance' in a pupil's life can effect immense change. Cooper *et al.* (1994), discussing the concept of resignification, also show how the individual pupil's behaviour can be altered when he or she ascribes 'significance' to a particular adult. Teachers can and frequently are such adults, because of their ability to provide engaging opportunities for pupils to make progress in learning.

To dwell on cause without relating it to planning for future teaching can only detract from the purpose of teaching, it may also cause the teacher to overlook the effects he or she can have, even in very difficult situations. This is not to minimise the challenge posed by individual pupils' emotional and behavioural difficulties; on the contrary, facing those difficulties teachers need to understand their potential for enabling pupils to achieve in well-managed classrooms.

In exploring the understanding of behaviour, the core question is one of understanding why behaviour occurs. Are human behaviours driven by inner forces described as cognition, biological impulses, the mind, or are they the result of external forces described as cultural, social, familial? These have often been represented in dychotomous terms as heredity and environment. Put starkly, is the behaviour a pupil displays a remit of his or her 'nature' or the 'nurturing' he or she has experienced. It is generally agreed that neither of these extremes explains behaviours. It is some combination of them which is seen as providing the best explanations.

There are a variety of views as to which holds most sway over behaviour: nurture or nature. However, there is a common view that it is not an 'additive' mixture, but rather a multiplier effect. Thus it is not as simple as being born with 'natural' characteristics to which 'nurture' is added, but rather a series of interactions between nature and nurture which results in ways of behaving.

That said, there are a variety of ways reflected by, and within, the different professional groups involved with children and young people for understanding their behaviour. In pursuing these understandings it is as well to remember that the perspectives which make most sense to the individual may be those which are closest to the individual's belief and value systems as to what it is to be human and what controls and affects our behaviours.

The major perspectives are those which focus upon:

- biological/medical;
- psychological;
- sociological;
- religious/cultural factors.

Most researchers and commentators, whilst favouring one or other of these perspectives, will nonetheless acknowledge that the others also have an effect. Thus behaviour is not seen as either/or in its causation; rather it is a mixture of perspectives which can provide insights into understanding and explaining that behaviour.

Before going on to explore the psychological perspective I am taking a brief glance at the other perspectives – brief because, whilst they may play important roles in behaviour, the factors they highlight are rarely under the control of teachers. This is not to lessen the importance for teachers of having at the very least an awareness of them. Rather it is to emphasise the importance of psychological perspectives for the understanding of teaching and learning.

The biological/medical perspective perceives normal behaviour as largely governed by genetic and/or chemical balances. This perspective sees misbehaviour, particularly challenging behaviour, in terms of faulty biology, chemical imbalances or failure of certain parts of the brain to operate normally. This perspective carries more controversy than others. Currently there is a resurgence of interest in this explanation for behaviour, the most documented area of which is attention deficit hyperactivity disorder (ADHD). Cooper and Ideus (1996) give a reasoned overview of this partic- ular syndrome and on the value of acknowledging the role that biology can play. Their defence of drug therapy used in conjunction with other interventions outlines roles for teachers in assisting pupils to change their behaviours.

Some of the insights afforded by the sociological perspectives on behaviour resonate with the psychological, particularly the ecosystemic perspective (see below for a description). The sociological perspective is perhaps most apparent in current notions of social exclusion and inclusion which are a central platform of the Government's policies. Sociological per- spectives understand behaviour in terms of structures and systems within society, and how individuals acquire meaning and value within them which shapes their behaviours. In this there are resonances with the notion of 'belongingness' (briefly discussed below), put forward initially by Maslow (1943). They perhaps have most to say in understanding how and why schools exclude pupils and pupils absent themselves from schools. As such they are outside the narrower scope of this book.

There are multitudes of religious and cultural explanations for behaviour. The ability to shed insight upon understanding behaviour relies more here than for other perspectives on the degree to which the belief and values espoused by a particular religious/cultural perspective are in accord with the person seeking to understand the behaviour. If his or her view of humanity accords with, for example, the Christian notion of original sin, the management of behaviour by a teacher within the classroom may well rely upon strategies that inculcate these beliefs in pupils to the extent that they adopt certain behaviour patterns rather than others. There will also be more overt expectations of certain behaviour patterns.

The psychological perspective

The predominant perspective for understanding behaviour within an education context is that of the psychological. This perspective divides into a number of sub-perspectives each having their own apologists. Ayers *et al.* (1995) give four broad sub-perspectives which are a useful framework for understanding the psychological perspective. They are:

- behavioural;
- cognitive-behavioural;
- ecosystemic;
- psychodynamic.

Ayers *et al.* (1995) provide excellent introductions to these perspectives. In this short volume there is only space to briefly mention their salient features.

The behavioural perspective

The behavioural perspective treats behaviour as a learnt response to stimuli. It considers only the observable part of behaviour, and works from the premise that only the observable is knowable. Assessment of behaviour is via checklist and observation schedules. From a behaviourist viewpoint, challenging behaviour is caused by maladaptive learning that results in incorrect responses to stimuli or poor stimuli that provoke the wrong responses. To change this behaviour the behaviourist will advocate programmes aimed at obtaining more appropriate responses from the stimuli given. In managing behaviour in classrooms this perspective would seek to negotiate contracts with pupils, and would establish reward systems which were linked to reinforcement programmes. Leading proponents of this understanding of behaviour and its implications for teachers are Kazdin (1994) Merrett (1993) and Wheldall (1992).

The cognitive-behavioural perspective

The cognitive-behavioural perspective takes into account the thought processes of the person; it perceives behaviour as being mediated through cognitive processes. Thus to understand behaviour one must gain an understanding of a person's perception of events, his or her beliefs about the environment they are in, and the thought process in which he or she arrives at a particular behaviour. This is achieved by requiring pupils to keep logs where their diaries and self-report on events are seen as useful for gaining insight into why the behaviour occurred. The emphasis is upon the thinking processes of the individual; the challenging behaviour being caused by maladaptive thinking. To change the behaviour, you must change the thinking process. This is managed within the classroom by seeking to place behaviour in a problem-solving context where alternative possible behaviours are derived from an analysis of the situation. The subsequent likely outcomes of these behaviours are also made apparent. Pupils are also encouraged to self-regulate by setting targets and monitoring their achievements: the less achieved, the more reflection on changes in the thinking process is required. Kendall and Braswell (1993) and Walker and Shea (1991) are among those who would advocate this perspective in understanding behaviour.

The ecosystemic perspective

The ecosystemic perspective is put forward by Cooper (1993), Cooper *et al.* (1994) and others. It seeks to understand behaviour as a series of interactions within and between people. Its theoretical base lies in systems analysis and the work of family therapists. This perspective argues that to understand the behaviour of the individual, observation of these interactions must be placed alongside interviews of the players taking part in the behaviour. Interactions that are perceived by players in negative terms result in cycles of inappropriate behaviour being set up which, unless more positive interactions occur, become self-perpetuating. Ayers *et al.* (1995) give a succinct description of the various interventions which this perspective would advocate in order to achieve successful management of behaviours in classrooms. Among them are ideas such as reframing, where through discussion or an exchange of views the pupil's and teacher's perception of the behaviour is reframed to arrive at a jointly perceived problem, rather than the problems being perceived as lying entirely with one of the players in the interaction. In this perspective the teacher needs to understand the cause of challenging behaviour as being the product of the interaction and thus not lying within the pupil, nor necessarily within the teacher. It is the nature of the interaction between teacher and pupil which is the cause of the problem behaviour, and thus it is the interaction which must be altered to achieve well-managed behaviour in the classroom.

The psychodynamic perspective

Lastly within the broad psychological understanding of behaviour there is the psychodynamic. This perspective draws upon the notion of consciousness and thus postulates an unconscious mind, which influences the more conscious behaviour. Behaviour, it maintains, is determined by conflicts between sections of the unconscious. It portrays problem behaviour as being driven by a lack of insight or awareness on the part of the individual of this unconscious conflict. The intervention strategies it puts forward are often difficult to put into practice in the classroom and this approach to understanding behaviour was not explored within the mainstream classrooms during the latter part of the twentieth century. It was seen as a 'specialist' approach, to be used with challenging behaviours in specialist settings. However, Greenhalgh (1994) puts forward a series of crosscurricular strategies with a focus upon personal and social education, that are derived from an understanding of behaviour from a largely psychodynamic perspective.

Applying the perspectives

The use of psychological understanding of behaviour in more general terms is explored by Leadbetter *et al.* (1999). They outline the variety of ways in which an understanding of a psychological perspective can provide useful tools for the teacher. Whilst they focus particularly on the impact psychology can have on learning, there are also suggestions on how these link to pupils' behaviours.

Running through some of these perspectives lies the notion of a hierarchy of needs as developed by Maslow (1943), and self-esteem and self-concept as put forward by Burns (1982) and Gurney (1988). This understanding of behaviour acknowledges certain biological needs such as warmth, food and shelter as basic, but goes on to postulate needs such as 'belongingness'. In this understanding of behaviour, once basic needs are met then the needs higher up the hierarchy come to the fore. The meeting of these needs affects the person's self-concept. Given feelings of low self-esteem in a particular area, they react to events, demands and requests within that area in ways which protect their self-esteem when they feel it is threatened further. This reaction often results in challenging behaviours, both those which cause disruption to others and those which are more internal and cause the pupil to be withdrawn.

The need to protect their self-esteem may also lead pupils to behave in ways which, while inappropriate for the teacher, are seen as appropriate by their peers. It is the relative significance the pupil places on peers and teachers which plays an important role in the behaviours the pupil chooses. Once the teacher obtains a position of significance in the eyes of the individual and class then the management of behaviour in the classroom becomes much easier.

The achievement of significance in the learning of pupils requires characteristics of and skills in:

- confidence;
- 'catching' pupils;
- curriculum;
- using learning support assistants;
- celebration;
- rule application;
- communication.

Confidence

A characteristic commonly witnessed in teachers with good classroom management is confidence. It is a difficult characteristic to describe in words or to set into a list of competencies. Its existence can be shown by describing where it comes from, what it requires for maintenance and how it can be sustained. One reason why confidence is so difficult to describe is because it is a feeling: you feel confident or not as the case may be. Its expression is recognised by pupils. Confidence is quiet in voice, sure in actions and purposeful in tasks.

The confident teacher is not the brash loud personality who seeks to impose authority by being louder in voice than the pupils. Indeed there is a saying within the profession that 'loud teachers have loud classes'. Using a quiet voice enables it to be used more effectively than the louder voice which is required from time to time. On the other hand, the quiet confident voice is not so quiet that the pupil cannot hear it! Being sure in action gives a sense to the pupil that the teacher is confident about the task in hand, that they are in charge of the situation. It is particularly important at the beginning and ending of lessons. A crisp start to lessons sets the pace of the lesson and generally gives the pupils the sense of purpose for the tasks to be achieved within the lesson.

Being hesitant at the start of a lesson creates space in which the pupils will find something else to occupy them. 'He who hesitates is lost' is a proverb worth bearing in mind when starting to teach.

Ending lessons is equally important in that it can provide pupils with the closure of learning that they need – closure in the sense of:

- being told what they have achieved/learnt;
- having time to quietly reflect upon that;
- getting ready for the next activity;
- gaining a sense of control, both imposed and self-control.

Whilst beginning and ending of lessons have been highlighted here, sureness of action is equally important during the lesson. It is needed when moving the learning, on and providing pace, progression and challenge.

Giving a sense of purpose to tasks is not achieved merely by ensuring that each task has a purpose, important as that is. Having a sense of purpose is more than the mere mechanical assigning of a purpose to a particular task.

Purpose is that ambience teachers create which imparts a sense of achievement of longer-term goals. Tasks by themselves can be repetitive, of a short duration, and may not *per se* convey any sense of long-term achievement or progress towards a larger goal. Purpose is closely allied to the longer-term progression the teacher wants pupils to achieve.

Confidence creates for pupils a sense of security in the teacher who is taking them through the curriculum. This level of confidence on the part of the teacher requires:

- knowledge of the subject;
- a desire to teach;
- realisation of authority.

Knowledge of the subject

In order to be confident in teaching, teachers need to have a secure knowledge of the subjects they are teaching. It is very difficult to teach confidently when you have little knowledge of the topic. Having a secure knowledge contributes to the well-planned lesson. It also provides the teacher with the necessary confidence in the classroom. Questions from pupils regarding the topic can then be answered with authority. This is not to argue that the teacher must know everything, but rather that the teacher's secure knowledge of the subject provides them with an understanding of their limitations, as well as the confidence to not always have to give 'the answer'. Knowing the subject includes how to gain access to that knowledge. It may not always be appropriate for the teacher to give 'the answer'; it may be more appropriate on occasions for the teacher to direct the pupil(s) in how to obtain the answer.

Knowledge of the subject can provide teachers with insights into how pupils are arriving at answers and conclusions in their work, and thus the validity of that procedure. This perhaps is most obvious when pupils give verbal answers to teachers' questions. Teachers use questions in many different ways; among them are questions used to probe pupils' understanding of a topic. Pupils can give answers which show ways of processing information which gives the 'right' answer – but without using the 'process' which the teacher had taught. Pupils can also give the 'wrong' answer which reveals a lack of understanding or misunderstanding of the processes required to arrive at the 'right' answer.

In both cases teachers' reactions to the pupil can be crucial in behavioural terms. If the teacher holds the view that the wrong answer inevitably means that the pupil is at fault, there will be a tendency to admonish the pupil. In fact it may be the case that the pupil's answers provide an insight into the process the pupil is using and how that can be used to positive effect. Rather than responding to the pupil with negative comments about their learning skills (you did not listen; you have not read the instructions properly etc), the teacher with secure subject knowledge is able to react by indicating where the pupils' process in answering the question throws light on alternative ways of achieving the answer or which aspect of process in achieving an answer needs to be addressed. The behavioural response from pupils receiving these forms of responses from teachers are more likely to be positive.

Desire to teach

It is axiomatic that the confident teacher wants to teach. The issue for many teachers is the degree to which they feel they are teaching and the degree to which they feel they are performing administrative and bureaucratic functions which they perceive as not contributory to their teaching. As the paperwork takes over as the focus of a teacher's work so it is seen as further divorcing the teacher from the time needed to address the behaviour management tasks in teaching. While there are occasions when administrative and bureaucratic demands have little to do with the classroom, most tasks which may be perceived as just filling in paper do in fact have a contribution to make to the quality of teaching and learning in the classroom. The question when dealing with administrative tasks is to ask how they assist in supporting pupils' achievements. Having teaching as the primary focus enables teachers to ensure that the administration and necessary paperwork supports learning rather than any other purpose.

The reluctant teacher will have problems in achieving a well-managed classroom. Teaching involves leadership; reluctance in teaching will show itself in the lack of confidence the teacher reveals in providing that leadership. Adults faced with a reluctant leader may rally round and provide support for that leader; pupils faced with the reluctant teacher tend not to do this. Sensing a vacuum, that the lack of wanting to teach provides, they will fill it with inappropriate behaviours.

Authority

As indicated, a teacher is *in* authority and also *an* authority but not necessarily *the* authority. Being in authority is a given responsibility and, within the UK, a legal responsibility of teachers. It brings with it notions of *in loco parentis*, acting in the best interests of the child as a good parent would. However, this authority is not a 'cloak of armour' put on in the staffroom just before the teacher leaves to enter the classroom. It is no longer possible, even if it was thought desirable, for teachers (as with other professional groups in society at large) to assume that they have authority in the eyes of their pupils simply by virtue of being a teacher.

The authority that a teacher has and builds up has to be maintained by exercising it in a collaborative manner. Collaboration means working with pupils to ensure that the teacher's authority is maintained. That authority rests upon a sense of fairness, clarity and explicitness: fairness which takes account, when appropriate, of pupils' views; clarity and explicitness in relation to the implication of that authority (see the section on communication below).

Sustaining confidence

Confidence needs sustaining by reflection and the building of evidence-based practice. The latter has been discussed earlier. The term 'reflection' here is being used to emphasise the need to realise and hold on to success.

When teaching it is easy to lose sight of the successful because the unsuccessful experiences come to the fore, as indicated when discussing challenging behaviour. Gaining a sense of successful teaching will enable a teacher to build his or her confidence, particularly in addressing the achievement of a class whose behaviour is focused upon learning.

'Catching' pupils

In achieving good classroom management pupils need to be engaged in their learning. Engagement is achieved in the many ways outlined above and in what follows. This section outlines some of the strategies which teachers can use to engage pupils.

The initial catching of pupils' attention creates a sound basis from which to manage classroom behaviour. This can be done in a number of ways; two important ones are promptness and structured routines. Being late for the start of a lesson, when committed by pupils, often results in some form of sanction being applied. When committed by a teacher, the result is often not a sanction but the challenge of restoring order in the classroom. Promptness on the part of a teacher conveys a number of positive messages: the importance of the lesson, the valuing of pupils' time and a sense of being organised, amongst them. It also leaves pupils with little or no time to engage in behaviours which would have to be eradicated when the teacher arrives.

Along with promptness is the need to have 'structures' which convey to pupils that the lesson has started. A prompt arrival at the lesson, coupled with a confident crisp start to it (discussed earlier) gives pupils a clear delineation between 'social time' and 'lesson time'. Pupils in these circumstances have a clear break which can enable them to focus upon the tasks in hand. Promptness also aids the gaining of pupils' attention. Some lessons may begin with pupils coming in and quietly getting on with tasks which have been set previously, where the pupils have well-developed study skills and have achieved a measure of independent learning. Pupils do not achieve this without acquiring learning routines laid down by the class teacher.

Teachers need to establish clear routines for such features of teaching as returning pupils' work, giving out materials and books, pupils' movement within the classroom, starting the lesson with every pupil's attention, storing equipment for access by pupils when appropriate. These aspects of classroom management will vary in their importance from subject to subject and within subjects from topic to topic. Lack of routines can produce the disorganised class which lends itself to challenging behaviours on the part of pupils.

This is not to advocate that routines should be inflexible. Indeed a change in a routine can have the effect of making pupils take particular note of a point a teacher wishes to make. The routines and structures give teachers a 'touchstone', which can be used when a pupil's behaviour disrupts the general pattern of learning in the class. For example, if the routine is that permission is sought before moving around a room or obtaining material/equipment from storage, then the pupils can be referred to the routine when they do not follow it and their behaviour is inappropriate or challenging. The routine does not have to have the formal status of a rule; it is a way 'we do things'.

Pleasant surroundings are more conducive to good behaviour than dreary, bleak, unstimulating ones. In times of financial stringency this may not always be easy to achieve. Some classrooms may bear the scars of many years of teaching and learning, some of which have not always been related to academic achievement. Graffiti-strewn desks and walls are not support-ive of the creation of a learning environment. Classroom displays of work can do much to make even these classrooms attractive pleasant places to work in. Pupils' work, well displayed, and frequently refreshed, helps to pro-vide a sense of pride and belonging which will support positive behaviour. Some pupils may find it difficult to have their work on display, perhaps coming from situations where this has not been a part of their experience. Some may under-rate their efforts, not able to cope with the praise implicit in having their work displayed. However, most pupils respond positively and even those pupils who find it difficult, can learn to accept and want their work displayed in classrooms where the teacher establishes this as a routine.

Another aspect of 'catching' pupils is teacher mobility. Where teachers confine themselves to one area of the classroom, such as a desk or being always near the board, pupils can develop behaviours in 'their' spaces. Good classroom management requires mobility while teaching, constantly moving from group to group within the classroom, ensuring that all the pupils are involved in the lesson. This movement also enables teachers to acquire other pieces of information. For example are there 'dead spots' within the classroom where pupils cannot hear as well as in other areas? Do some areas of the classroom lend themselves more easily to differing activities? Some areas may be better lit than others. These and other physical aspects of the classroom can affect pupils' ability to see, listen or move about in response to the teaching they are receiving.

Another aspect of 'catching' pupils lies in seating arrangements. Some grouping of pupils within the class may be the source of behaviours which, though minor, can lead to more challenging behaviour, because they easily distract the pupils and the teacher from the purpose of the lesson. Moving pupils and rearranging seating can be a simple and yet powerful strategy for enabling pupils to remain on task and to rise to positive expectations from teachers.

Curriculum

Pupils with challenging behaviours are entitled to the broad and balanced curriculum made available for all pupils. Denying pupils access to this curriculum on the basis of their behaviour is to risk an escalation of the problem behaviours. The challenge is to provide a diverse curriculum, which maintains the pupils' right to a broad and balanced curriculum. Creating different curricular areas for pupils from their peers is to create alternative curricula. The danger here is the perception of 'worthwhileness' pupils assign to this alternative. Alternative curricula must not attract a lower status than that offered to these pupils' peers. Of particular importance is the status given to the accreditation gained by the pupils; these need to be celebrated in a manner which gives them equal importance to accreditations often perceived as being more academic. Managing challenging behaviour by constructing groups who follow different curricular areas is not always the answer to a teacher's problems managing a class. A further exacerbating factor in managing these groups is often the loss of good behaviour models for pupils to aspire to. When all the pupils with challenging behaviours are placed together the range of good models of behaviours the pupils' experience can dramatically narrow.

Acknowledging these issues it is necessary from time to time to construct for individual pupils a particular curriculum 'diet'; in doing so it is important not to narrow the curriculum they experience.

Cole *et al.* (1998) found that the subject content of much of the national curriculum was seen as appropriate for pupils with emotional and behavioural difficulties. What they found difficult was the issue of relevance of that content to the lives of pupils. Teachers frequently assume that the relevance of the knowledge, skill and/or understanding they are teaching is obvious. Pupils' behavioural responses to lessons may stem from not perceiving this relevance. Teachers need to relate the learning intentions of lessons to their pupils' lives, their aspirations and goals, thereby giving the curriculum a relevance. Pupils who challenge need constant reiteration of the reasons for learning which relate to their lives.

Having established the purpose and reason for the learning task there is a need to establish that pupils have the skills necessary to engage in the tasks. Often pupils who challenge have limited abilities, particularly undeveloped problem-solving and communication skills. A response to these educational needs which focuses solely upon teaching the basic literacy and numeracy skills isolated from the whole curriculum is likely to have limited success. An approach which seeks to enable pupils to gain these skills within the subjects of a broad and balanced curriculum will have greater success. Enabling pupils to acquire these skills at their point of application provides a motivating purpose and relevance for their acquisition.

Where pupils are identified as being challenging in behaviour terms, they have often reached a point where they are failing to engage with the curriculum being offered. This point can be reached early in a pupil's school career. Finding achievement in academic learning difficult can quickly result in pupils finding alternative ways of gaining recognition which results in their being disengaged from education.

To re-engage them and give them some ownership of their learning is important if they are not to be a continuing behaviour management problem for the teacher. This requires curriculum planning to contain flexibility in order to set achievable targets for individual pupils. Negotiation of these targets can provide pupils with some responsibility and ownership of their learning. As indicated earlier, the more pupils re-engage with the tasks within the classroom the less will be the behavioural challenges that they present.

Pupils whose behaviour challenges teachers often have low self-esteem as academic learners and few skills for assessing their own progress. A strategy which involves in an overt manner pupils assessing their work can enable them to gain a sense of progression. From feeling they are unable to learn they can begin the process of seeing themselves as successful learners. Pupils who see themselves as successful learners are a hallmark of the well-managed classroom.

Learning support assistants

The numbers of learning support assistants (LSAs) in classrooms is on the increase. Many schools also have voluntary workers who are used to support pupils in classes. Some schools use a 'buddy' or 'mentor' system. This is where an older pupil is assigned a young pupil as a 'friend' and provides them with support in learning. The benefits of having extra adults and/or young people in the classroom should extend beyond the usefulness of having just another pair of hands. OFSTED (1996) found that where this form of support is effective, behaviour problems were lessened and academic achievement was raised.

To use LSAs and others effectively within the classroom the teacher needs to ensure:

- they are made aware of the lessons plans and outcomes;
- they are aware of and implement the behaviour conventions the class teacher has set so that pupils experience a consistency of approach;

- the sharing of the high expectations that the teacher has of his or her pupils;
- that they know the parameters of the functions the teacher has for them.

In this way they can provide not only the learning support but also coherence in the management of the class and an additional model of acceptable behaviour.

Celebration

A powerful motivator for behaving well is to receive an acknowledgement that one is doing so. Celebrating good behaviour is an activity teachers do less often than pointing out poor behaviour. There are a variety of ways positive celebration can be conducted, including:

- recording;
- orally;
- marking;
- accreditation.

Recording pupils' achievements, both academic and behavioural in visible ways by means of a star chart, or 'completion of tasks' chart, is one way of enabling pupils not only to see their progression but also to see their achievement of a goal over a period of time. It engenders a feeling of success which can provide motivation for staying on task. Sharing the records of marks contained within a teacher's mark book may be an alternative method. Where a degree of privacy is deemed necessary, giving pupils 'stickers' for achievement which they can stick in a booklet or folder is yet another way of using records to support pupils' good behaviour. Some schools will use these records to award a certificate once particular goals are achieved, doing this in a public manner in assemblies.

Teachers' recognition of pupil behaviour is often limited to when it challenges or strays from the teacher's expectations. This recognition is necessary, since it gives the pupil an indication of the teacher's awareness of the situation, enables them to form a judgement as to the likely consequences of continuing that course of action and reminds them that there is a purpose to the lesson. However, if the sole communication pupils receive are instructions related to the purpose of the lesson and a 'rebuke' when they stray from that purpose, their motivation to remain on task is likely to lessen.

Pupils need to be praised when behaving well and when they are engaged in learning. This praise needs to be appropriately given and not given when undeserved. Catching pupils being thoughtful, kind, supportive of others, concentrating on the task in hand, making an effort to present their work well, and giving these activities recognition helps to build the positive relationships which underpin good classroom management.

This recognition can be founded on pupils' work. Completion of a piece of work leads teachers to assess it and award a mark. Often this is accompanied by a curt word or two, 'good', 'better', 'not your best'. Given the time pressures that teachers may be under this is understandable. However, for pupils who challenge this often becomes a meaningless phrase, particularly if they rarely receive suggestions and positive comments. A more extended comment can convey to the pupil the message that he or she is valued, in particular that the personal effort made is being recognised. It may only be a small effort yet its recognition encourages the pupil to continue and extend it. A strategy used by some teachers is to develop their range of positive comments so that they can vary them. This can have the effect of getting pupils to take the process of marking as an interactional event, rather than an end in itself. It is not unknown for teachers to end their comments with a question which invites an answer from the pupil, furthering their engagement in their learning.

Rule application

Within or alongside a school's behaviour policy there will be some school rules. These will cover behavioural expectations within the school as a whole. Teachers should tailor their within-classroom rules so that they 'nest' within these wider school rules, and provide a 'coherence' for the pupils who need to operate within them.

Teachers cannot assume pupils have a knowledge of the rules, particularly at the start of a year or when they first meet a class. Nor should they assume that the reasons for their particular rules are apparent. Rules can appear very arbitrary to pupils, particularly when they have been imposed, rather than derived after some consideration of pupils' views as to what rules are for and thus what rules are needed.

Rules can provide support in managing behaviour by:

* setting parameters of acceptable behaviours;
* reinforcing the goals of learning;
* giving 'value' to the pupils.

In agreeing a set of rules pupils can assimilate a set of values and norms which they can internalise. They can move from a dependency on the rules set as the parameters of acceptable behaviour to a position where they achieve self-discipline. This is greatly helped by having rules which they have had some say in forming and which are seen as supportive of the goals of teaching and learning.

Long lists of rules tend to be self-defeating, as they invite pupils to find a behaviour not covered by them. Glasser (1998) argues that they should be kept short and be based upon principles of 'human justice', such as fairness, respect for others, and tolerance. Knight (1991) proposed that they should be written in terms of rights and responsibilities for each of the players in the class. Thus he proposes a set of rights and responsibilities for pupils and a separate list for the teacher. These have the merit of making explicit the reasons for the behavioural expectations the teacher has of his or her pupils, and also what pupils can expect from their teacher. Pupils whose behaviour is a challenge often do not have this form of framework to govern their behaviours, and can initially find such explicitness difficult to assimilate. They may be very vocal as to what they perceive as their rights, but not quite so ready to accept responsibilities.

Once rules have been agreed they should be consistently applied. Porter (2000) indicates that this consistency should be seen at three levels:

* a constant expectation across time;
* maintaining standards for all students;
* applying consequences consistently.

Consequences and sanctions

Jones and Jones (1998) make the point that teachers have two different approaches to pupils' errors, seeing errors in academic learning as more legitimate than those in behaviour. For example teachers often assume that mistakes in learning are made because the pupil has not understood the task, or how to achieve a particular outcome. Whereas with errors in behaviours, the teacher can be quick to assume that the pupil is deliberately misbehaving and that they should implicitly know how to behave. This observation serves as a reminder that behaviour has to be learnt and pupils can make genuine errors in learning how to behave as they do in learning how to learn. It can be important for teachers to check the pupils' understanding of their behaviour before applying a sanction.

The application of sanctions should conform to the school policy and:

- be planned for;
- be applied consistently and with equity;
- apply to the act and not the actor;
- enable cause and effect to be understood.

Teachers should ensure that their familiarity and knowledge of the school's behaviour policy extends to the guidance it contains on the range and application of sanctions allowed. This may be obvious, but it is important for teachers and pupils that any sanctions given conform to the policy of the school.

Teachers with well-managed classrooms have planned the sanctions they will use as carefully as they have planned other aspects of their lessons. This prevents them from issuing the threat of a sanction they subsequently find they cannot apply. Telling a pupil that he or she will be requested to stay behind after a lesson, only to find that an appointment elsewhere means that the teacher cannot enforce it, will do little for the credibility of the teacher. Planning for sanctions will also provide a focus for the prevention of their use. Teaching and learning will be considerably less successful if the sole motivation for pupils is the avoidance of sanctions. If pupils live with the fear of sanctions what they will learn is how to avoid them rather than experiencing the success that comes from achieving the learning outcome.

Sanctions should be applied consistently but with equity. Equity in application is required to meet any mitigating circumstances which may be a part of the misdemeanours or the reasons why a pupil has committed them. Pupils have a keen sense of fairness and will carry some resentment if they perceive one of their peers is being treated unfairly by teachers. Sanctions applied with a rigid consistency without a discrimination based upon any mitigating circumstances will do little to sustain the building of positive relationships between teachers and pupils.

Sanctions need to be applied specifically because of an action or inaction on the part of the pupil. This may need to be made very explicit if teachers are to avoid the accusation from a pupil that they are being 'picked on'. It is the act which needs to be the focus of the sanction. In applying the sanction it is important not to label the pupil. Statements such as 'You are a liar and this will happen' do little more than confirm to the pupil the teacher's perception of them as liars. Statements which address the act of lying and link the sanction to the action provide some protection of the pupil's self-esteem; they also enable the pupil to gain an understanding of cause and effect and provide the pupil with an opportunity to change their actions. This approach will also give some rationale for the particular sanction being applied. The act of lying having been caused by a particular set of behaviours, the sanction being applied could be constructed to enable the pupil to make some retribution and/or learn how to behave more appropriately on a subsequent occasion. This latter may require some discussion between pupil and teacher as outlined in the section on challenging behaviour. (See Long 2000 for a more detailed exposition of understanding and dealing with lying.)

Communication

If there is a 'glue' which holds all the various strategies together, and is an integral aspect of each one of them, then it is the clarity of the communication between teachers and pupils.

One constant theme of this book is that to manage behaviour in classrooms those involved need to communicate their expectation of each other. Clarity in communication is important if pupils are to understand the expectations the teacher has of them. Teachers will usually have total clarity regarding what they have said, but pupils on the receiving end of the communication may receive a very different message, because the received communication has not made sense to them. Thus clarity in communication is not achieved solely by teachers speaking clearly, it requires teachers to monitor how pupils receive and interpret what is said. Pupils' behaviour can be a response to what they interpret the teacher to have said, rather than what the teacher believes he or she communicated.

Much is also conveyed in communicating with pupils. It is frequently very salutary to watch a video recording of yourself teaching and to listen not only to what is being said, but to how; the tone, modulation, pitch and volume used all convey meaning to pupils. The simple statement 'I want you to begin to work now' taken at face value has a simple meaning; there is some work which you can start at this moment. However, vary the tone, emphasis, volume and pitch and a variety of meanings can accompany the statement, from 'I am not going to wait any longer because you are wasting time, begin now' to 'I am interested in seeing if you can complete this task and how you do so'. For pupils with challenging behaviours it is often these aspects of communication which are more important than the simple surface message. Among the reasons for this is the fact that these aspects of communication convey the values, beliefs and attitudes the teacher has towards them, as well as the emotional context of the situation.

Two further aspects of verbal communication impact upon pupils' behaviours: sequencing and length of instruction, and range of vocabulary. Pupils often find they are faced with a set of verbal instructions from the teacher, frequently at the start of the lesson. If these are too long pupils can forget parts of them, and if they are given out of the sequence in which they must be done pupils can quickly become confused. Examples at adult levels of problems in communication abound; perhaps the most common one is the giving and receiving of telephone numbers. The message left on the answerphone rattles off the number of the caller with the request to phone them back. The caller leaving the number is totally familiar with it but the receiver is often left struggling to remember it, write it down and check the sequence. Recently when the initial 01 became 02 the receiver has had to double check because the expected start to the sequence is 01 – can 02 be right?

This example also illustrates the need for teachers to ensure that the range of vocabulary used is understood. Requesting a pupil to place his posterior upon the horizontal plane that will support his body while he settles down to apply himself to some cognitive labours, may well stretch the range of his vocabulary, but at the risk of him not actually sitting down and completing a task. An important aspect of learning is acquiring new concepts with their attended vocabulary and understanding the different ways words can be used. Each subject has its own vocabulary and can use commonly used words in specific ways. Think for example of the meanings of 'mean', or the use of 'fair'. Pupils without these understandings can misunderstand or not understand what is expected of them with the result that their behaviours are not the ones the teacher believes he or she has requested.

A further point regarding communication in relation to managing behaviour in classrooms is understanding body language. Neill and Caswell (1993) point to the fact that pupils and teachers are constantly interpreting each other's body language: the way we sit, stand, where we are in relation to others, how we present ourselves, for example, have powerful influences on the behaviours which we display. Where pupils are sitting up straight, making eye contact with their teacher, they are deemed to be concentrating upon the task in hand, whilst being laid back, slouched in the chair fiddling with a pen is more often interpreted as not caring or listening to the teacher. The point here is not whether either of these caricatures is correct, but to highlight the fact that teachers make interpretations of pupils' body language which may not be correct, and thus it is important to check gently and care-fully when making judgements based on observations as to the actual state of mind of the pupils concerned.

Conclusion

The contents of this book were written with the newly qualified teacher and those in initial teacher training in mind. It has outlined a number of factors which contribute to good classroom management and meeting the educational needs of the pupils who have difficulties in settling down easily to academic learning under the direction of a teacher.

It has not portrayed itself as having all the answers. As elucidated at the outset, not all the approaches it examines work in all situations with all pupils. Indeed some of the strategies it suggests may not be possible in some situations.

What it aimed to do was to set out the issues and to invite teachers to reflect upon them in relation to a particular pupil or group of pupils they are familiar with, to assess to what extent they have applicability to their practice and then to try some of them out.

Though written under separate headings, the ideas should be taken as an integrated whole. The basic premise has been that it is difficult to separate achieving well-managed behaviour in classes without addressing teaching issues more widely. Behaviour should not be seen as separate from learning.

If the book has enabled the reader to reflect upon their view of what constitutes teaching and how they might enhance their skills in managing and understanding behaviour it will have achieved its modest aims.

Further reading

These are sources I have found particularly useful and that expand some of the concepts I have outlined.

Greenhalgh, P. (1994) *Emotional Growth and Learning*. London: Routledge.

Maines, B. and Robinson, G. (1992) *A Bag of Tricks*. Bristol: Lucky Duck Publishing.

O'Brien, T. (1998) *Promoting Positive Behaviour*. London: David Fulton Publishers.

Porter, L. (2000) *Behaviour in Schools: Theory and Practice for Teachers*. Buckingham: Open University Press.

Smith, C. and Laslett, R. (1993) *Effective Classroom Management: A Teacher's Guide*. London: Routledge.

Visser, J. and Rayner S (eds) (1999) *Emotional and Behavioural Difficulties: A Reader*. Lichfield: QEd Publications.

References

Ashworth, A. (1998) *Once in a House on Fire*. London: Picador.

Axline, V. (1966) *Dibs: In Search of Self*. London: Gollancz.

Ayers, H., Clarke, D. and Murray, A. (1995) *Perspectives on Behaviour*. London: David Fulton Publishers.

Bowers, T. (1996) 'Putting the 'E' back in EBD', *Emotional and Behavioural Difficulties* **1** (1), 8–13.

Brown, S. and McIntyre, K. (1993) *Making Sense of Teaching*. Buckingham: Open University Press.

Burns, R.B. (1982) *Self-Concept Development and Education*. London: Holt.

Charlton, T. and David, K. (1993) *Managing Misbehaviour in Schools*. London: Routledge.

Cole, T., Visser, J. and Upton, G. (1998) *Effective Schooling for Pupils with Emotional and Behavioural Difficulties*. London: David Fulton Publishers Publishers.

Cooper, P. (1993) *Effective Schools for Disaffected Pupils: Integration and Segregation*. London: Routledge.

Cooper, P. (1996) 'Giving it a name: the value of descriptive categories in educational approaches to emotional and behavioural difficulties', *Support for Learning* **6** (1), 22–6.

Cooper, P. and Ideus, K. (1996) *Attention Deficit Hyperactivity Disorder: A Practical Guide for Teachers*. London: David Fulton Publishers.

Cooper, P., Smith, C. and Upton, G. (1994) *Emotional and Behavioural Difficulties: Theory into Practice*. London: Routledge.

Cornwall, J. and Tod, J. (1998) *Emotional and Behavioural Difficulties*. London: David Fulton Publishers.

Creese, A., Daniels, H. and Norwich, B (1997) *Teacher Support Teams in Primary and Secondary Schools*. London: David Fulton Publishers.

Daniels, H., Visser, J. and Cole, T. (in press) 'Values and behaviour in education: an activity theory approach to research' in Kurohelatti, M. (ed.) *Report of the First International EBD Colloquium Joensuu,* Finland: The University of Joensuu.

Daniels, H. *et al.* (1998) *Emotional and Behavioural Difficulties in Mainstream Schools: Research Report RR90.* London: Department for Education and Employment.

DES (1989) *Discipline in Schools: The Elton Report.* London: HMSO.

DfE (1994) *The Education of Pupils With Emotional and Behavioural Difficulties.* (Circular 9/94) London: Department for Education.

DfEE (1997) *Excellence for All Children: Meeting Special Educational Needs (Green Paper).* London: The Stationery Office.

DfEE (1999) *Social Inclusion: Pupil Support.* London: Department for Education and Employment.

DfEE (2000) *Consultation on Revised SEN Code of Practice on the Identification and Assessment of Pupils with SEN and SEN Thresholds.* London: Department for Education and Employment.

Engestrom, Y. (1996) *Perspectives on Activity Theory.* Cambridge: Cambridge University Press.

Farrell, P. (1995) 'Emotional and behavioural difficulties: causes, definitions and assessment', in Farrell, P. (ed.) *Children with Emotional and Behavioural Difficulties – Strategies for Assessment and Intervention.* London: Falmer.

Glasser, W. (1998) *The Quality School: Managing Students without Coercion.* New York: Harper Perennial.

Gray, J. and Richer, J. (1988) *Classroom Responses to Disruptive Behaviour.* London: Routledge.

Greenhalgh, P. (1994) *Emotional Growth and Learning.* London: Routledge.

Gurney, P. (1988) *Self Esteem in Children with Special Educational Needs.* London: Routledge.

Jones, V.F. and Jones, L.S. (1998) *Comprehensive Classroom Management: Creating Communities of Support and Solving Problems.* Boston: Allyn & Bacon.

Kazdin, A (1994) *Behaviour Modification in Applied Settings.* Pacific Grove, CA: Brooks Publication.

Kendall, P. and Braswell, L. (1993) *Cognitive-Behaviour Therapy for Impulsive Children.* London: Guildford Press.

Knight, T. (1991) 'Democratic schooling: basis for a school code of behaviour', in Lovegrove, M. and Lewis, R. (eds) *Classroom Discipline.* Melbourne: Longman Cheshire.

Leadbetter, J. *et al.* (1999) *Applying Psychology in the Classroom.* London: David Fulton Publishers.

Long, R. (2000) *Children Who Lie.* Tamworth: NASEN.

Maras, P. (1996) 'Whose are the 'E's in EBD?', *Emotional and Behavioural Difficulties* 1 (1), 14–21.

Maslow, A. (1943) 'A theory of human motivation', *Psychological Review* **50**, 370–96.

McIntyre, K. (1995) 'Pastoral care and black pupils: an uneasy relationship', in Farrell, P. (ed.) *Children with Emotional and Behavioural Difficulties – Strategies for Assessment and Intervention.* London: Falmer.

Merrett, F. (1993) *Encouragement Works Best: Positive Approaches to Classroom Management.* London: David Fulton Publishers.

Morris, S. (1999) 'Working with difficult pupils: a case study of effectiveness', Unpublished PhD Thesis, The University of Birmingham.

Mortimore, P., Sammons, L., Stoll, L. and Ecob, R. (1988) *School Matters.* Wells: Open Books.

Neill, S. and Caswell, C. (1993) *Body Language for Competent Teachers.* London: Routledge.

OFSTED (1996) *Promoting High Achievement.* London: HMSO.

Porter, L. (2000) *Behaviour in Schools: Theory and Practice for Teachers.* Buckingham: Open University Press.

Rutter, M., Maughan, B., Mortimore, P. and Ouston, J. (1979) *Fifteen Thousand Hours.* London: Open Books.

Smith, C. and Laslett, R (1993) *Effective Classroom Management: A Teacher's Guide.* London: Routledge.

Walker, J. and Shea, T. (1991) *Behaviour Management.* London: Macmillan.

Wang, M.C. and Reynolds, M.C. (1995) *Making a Difference for Students at Risk: Trends and Alternatives.* Thousand Oaks, CA: Crown Press.

Wheldall, K. (1992) *Discipline in Schools: Psychological Perspectives on The Elton Report.* London: Routledge.